NORTH AMERICAN Pelicans

NORTH AMERICAN Pelicans

A Carolrhoda Nature Watch Book

written and photographed by Lynn M. Stone

Carolrhoda Books, Inc. / Minneapolis

For my parents, Charlotte and Mel, who introduced me to pelicans

Text and photographs copyright © 2003 by Lynn M. Stone

The photograph on page 41 is courtesy of Frans Lanting/Minden Pictures.

Carolrhoda Books, Inc.
A division of Lerner Publishing Group
241 First Avenue North
Minneapolis, MN 55401

Website address: www.lernerbooks.com

Library of Congress Cataloging-in-Publication Data

Stone, Lynn M.
    Pelicans / written and photographed by Lynn M. Stone.
        p.   cm.
    "A Carolrhoda nature watch book."
    Summary: Describes the physical characteristics, behavior, and habitat of pelicans.
    ISBN: 1–57505–171–0 (lib bdg. : alk. paper)
    1. Pelicans—Juvenile literature. [1. Pelicans.] I. Title.
QL696.P47 S76 2003
598.4'3—dc21   2001006943

Manufactured in the United States of America
1 2 3 4 5 6 – JR – 08 07 06 05 04 03

CONTENTS

Brown pelicans fish in the coastal waters of Florida.

6

A PELICAN DIVES

With wings folded and neck and bill extended, a brown pelican hurtles at 40 miles an hour (60 km/h) toward a school of fish swimming near the sea's surface. It knifes into the water.

When a brown pelican dives, only its head and neck go underwater. Air sacs in its neck and breast keep the pelican's body from submerging. The air sacs also soften the impact when the bird hits the water at high speed.

As it slashes into the sea, the pelican opens its foot-long (0.3-m-long) beak and the pouch attached below it. The soft pouch is the pelican's trademark. Made of thin, elasticized skin, the pouch is really a big fish scoop. The pelican's lower bill bends into a hoop to open the top of the pouch. The pouch expands when the seawater, with its load of fish, pours into it.

This brown pelican has raised its head to drain the water from its pouch.

After a dive, a brown pelican drains water from its pouch by lifting its head and tilting it forward. Water may drain for a full minute, but the pelican is patient; it doesn't want the fish to spill out.

When the pouch is water-free, the pelican tosses its head back and swallows its catch. The brown pelican will sometimes flip a fish up and out of its pouch, catching it on the way down. A pelican at rest usually keeps the pouch pulled in tight against its lower **mandible,** or beak.

Despite the pelican's effort, some small fish may escape in the flood of water coming from the pouch. That explains why gulls often flock close to fishing brown pelicans. Gulls will even land on a pelican's back or head to be sure to be near enough to catch any escaping fish.

Below: *A laughing gull wants to be close enough to catch any fish that might escape from the pelican's bill.*

The cormorant is a member of the same family of water-loving birds as the pelicans.

NORTH AMERICAN PELICANS, BROWN AND WHITE

The brown pelican is one of seven **species,** or kinds, of pelicans that live in many of the mild regions on every continent except Antarctica. They belong to a group of water-loving birds called **Pelecaniformes.** Besides pelicans, the group includes cormorants, anhingas, tropic birds, and frigate birds. All members of this group have four toes connected by webbing on each foot. And most Pelecaniformes have a bare throat pouch, although only pelicans have eye-popping, basket-sized pouches. Pelecaniformes, like many kinds of fish-eating birds, nest in large groups called **colonies.**

Three subspecies, or varieties, of brown pelicans live in North America. This is an eastern brown pelican.

The brown pelican is one of two pelican species that live in North America. Most **ornithologists,** the scientists who study birds, divide the brown pelicans into six subspecies, or varieties. Three of them—the eastern, the California, and the Caribbean—live in North America. The brown pelican subspecies all have similar habits, but they differ somewhat in size and color.

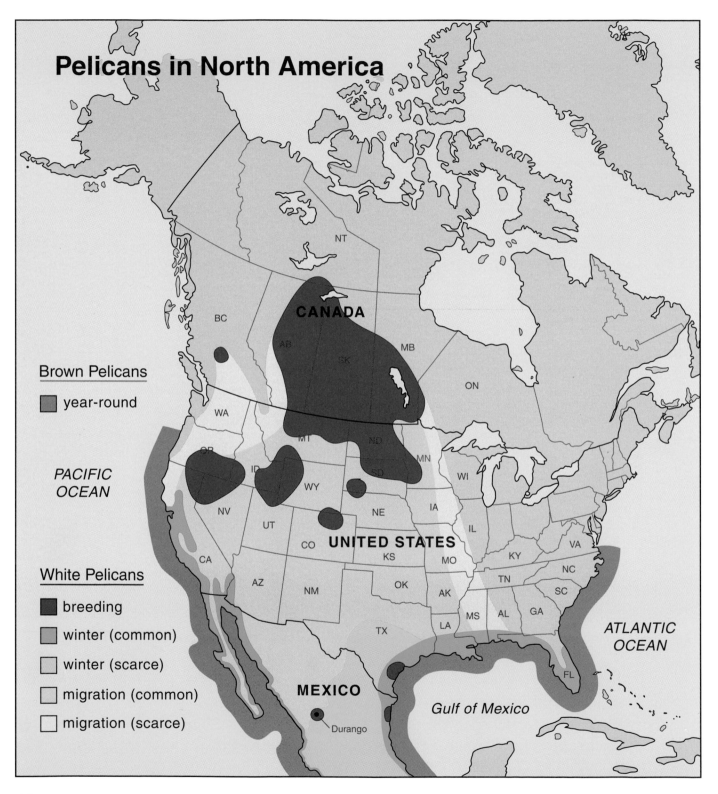

Pelicans in North America

Brown Pelicans

- ▩ year-round

PACIFIC OCEAN

White Pelicans

- ■ breeding
- ▩ winter (common)
- ▨ winter (scarce)
- ▨ migration (common)
- ☐ migration (scarce)

CANADA

UNITED STATES

MEXICO

Durango

Gulf of Mexico

ATLANTIC OCEAN

NT

BC

AB

SK

MB

ON

WA

OR

ID

MT

ND

MN

WY

SD

WI

NV

UT

NE

IA

IL

CO

KS

MO

KY

VA

CA

AZ

NM

OK

AK

TN

NC

SC

GA

MS

AL

LA

TX

FL

American white pelicans spend their summers on freshwater ponds in the western United States and Canada.

North America's other pelican is the American white. White pelicans are stunning birds, much bigger than their brown cousins. They are not as well known as the brown pelican because most of them spend much of their lives in freshwater lakes in the West, away from large human population centers. In contrast, brown pelicans are coastal birds. They live along the southern seacoasts of California and Florida, among other places, where millions of people see them.

13

The American white pelican is much larger than its cousin, the brown pelican.

Brown pelicans and American white pelicans share many habits and basically the same fishing gear—long necks, bills with a hooked tip on the upper mandible, pouches, stubby legs, and webbed feet. The stubby legs and flat, ducklike feet make great paddles when a pelican is afloat. They also help cushion the pelican's water landing. The stubby legs and webbed feet aren't made for running or power walking, though, so pelicans are clumsy on land.

FLIGHTS AND FEATHERS

Pelicans need dry land, such as a sandbar or an island shore or even a dock or pier, where they can **preen** and roost. When a pelican preens, it is cleaning and oiling its feathers. A pelican produces and stores oil in a gland at the base of its tail. It takes oil from the gland with the tip of its bill, then runs its bill through its feathers, using it like a pick or a comb.

Preening is a must for a pelican's sur-vival. Without constant attention, a pelican's feathers would become dirty and dry. Dirty, dry feathers absorb water more easily than clean feathers and become wet and heavy. Heavy, wet feathers lose their ability to **insulate,** or protect, a bird's body from cold air and water. They also make it difficult for the pelican to take off from land or water and to fly.

These white pelicans are preening. They are taking oil from a gland near their tails and using their bills to spread the oil through their feathers. Clean, well-oiled feathers protect pelicans from wet and cold.

Pelicans often raise their beaks to clear their throat when preening.

On a hot day, a roosting pelican may use its pouch to help cool off. It stretches the pouch so its surface is exposed like a wide, flat bag. Then the bird flutters or wiggles it. Extra body heat is released through the bare skin of the pouch, much as a panting dog releases heat through its mouth and tongue.

A male white pelican is one of the world's heaviest flying birds, although it weighs less than its bulk would suggest—just 10 to 17 pounds (5–8 kg). The average weight of a brown pelican is about 7 pounds (3 kg). Like other flying birds, a pelican has hollow bones to keep its weight low.

In flight, pelicans are majestic, whether flying like winged arrows, lazy kites, or military jets in formation. With wings outstretched, seldom flapping, pelicans can soar long distances like giant paper airplanes. They can circle upward in giant spirals to become sky confetti, or race along on invisible air rails a whisker above the wave crests.

To soar, pelicans take advantage of invisible air currents. Riding on these currents means they can fly with fewer flaps of their wings. They save energy this way, which means they don't have to spend as much time searching for food, the source of their energy.

When they're not soaring, pelicans have a slow, easy wing beat. Many small birds have to move their wings so quickly to stay airborne that they become a blur, but a pelican's wing strokes can easily be counted. Nevertheless, a pelican's relatively few wing strokes can propel it along at 25 to 35 miles (40–56 km) an hour. While flying, a pelican's keen eyes look for schools of fish below. When it spots a school, the brown pelican tilts its wings and rushes into a dive. The white pelican lowers itself in a more gradual descent.

A pelican can soar on wind currents and cover great distances with slow, easy wing beats.

PELICAN HABITATS

Brown pelicans and white pelicans rarely compete with each other for food or space. Brown pelicans generally fish in the open sea close to land. They seldom fly more than 20 miles (30 km) seaward for a meal. They especially like to fish in **estuaries,** the food-rich waters where rivers enter the sea, and in saltwater bays. Brown pelicans almost never fish in freshwater.

White pelicans are largely birds of freshwater marshes and lakes. For most of the year they depend on freshwater fish for food. During the cold months, many white pelican flocks winter in coastal areas, but even then they seek out quiet ocean bays or freshwater lakes for their fish. They rarely mingle with brown pelicans, except on the island beaches where both species rest and preen.

Brown pelicans fish in the open sea, close to the coast.

American white pelicans gather in large groups near freshwater lakes.

Brown pelicans thrive in coastal habitats, along both the Atlantic and Pacific coasts. On the Pacific coast of North America, brown pelicans are found from Mexico north into Oregon. They nest on sea islands off the coasts of Mexico and California.

Brown pelicans live along the Atlantic coast from North Carolina south to the tip of the Florida peninsula and into the Florida Keys. They also live along the Gulf of Mexico from Florida's west coast to Texas and Mexico. Brown pelicans also may be found on several islands in the Caribbean Sea, including Puerto Rico and the U.S. Virgin Islands.

Although white pelicans often spend winters in coastal areas, they are not residents there. Nearly all American white pelicans nest in 13 states, from Wisconsin west to California. They also nest in 5 Canadian provinces, from Ontario westward into Manitoba, Saskatchewan, Alberta, and British Columbia. The largest nesting colonies of American white pelicans anywhere are in Manitoba and Saskatchewan. North Dakota has the largest population of nesting white pelicans in the United States with about 12,000 birds. Occasionally, a small colony of white pelicans nests at a lake in Durango, Mexico, some 4,000 miles (6,000 km) south of the Canadian colonies.

This white pelican has caught a fish.

GOIN' FISHIN'

"Goin' fishin'" is a way of life for pelicans. Since they can't dive and swim underwater like their cormorant cousins, pelicans catch only fish that are swimming within 3 feet (1 m) of the water surface. That is as far underwater as a pelican can reach when its neck is fully extended.

Brown pelicans typically eat menhaden, mullet, pinfish, sea trout, anchovies, and sardines. In Florida, brown pelicans are known to eat at least 30 different species of saltwater fish. Occasionally brown pelicans gobble up shrimp.

White pelicans usually eat freshwater fish such as carp, chub, minnows, and bullheads. Sometimes they eat game fish, such as trout, bass, and bluegills.

White pelicans that nest at Chase Lake in North Dakota are known to eat mouthfuls of tiger salamanders.

Long ago, people believed that a pelican stored fish in its pouch, as if the pouch were a flying aquarium. In reality, a pelican stores fish in its stomach. The pouch is merely the tool to catch the fish.

That pouch is amazing, but does the pouch of a pelican, as a poet once wrote, "hold more than its bellycan"? For a few seconds, yes. A brown pelican's pouch scoops up about 2.5 gallons (9.5 l.) of water, far more weight and volume than its belly can hold. A white pelican's pouch holds even more. But a fishing pelican begins to drain water from its pouch immediately.

Skydiving brown pelicans are familiar sights, but brown pelicans don't always dive to fish. A pelican swimming near a silvery school of fish will stab its open beak, pouch extended, into them. That type of **lunge,** or fish-and-strike, fishing is similar to the way white pelicans fish, except white pelicans are more social than browns when they're fishing.

The pelican's amazing pouch is really a tool to help it catch fish.

Brown pelicans usually travel in flocks, but when they dive for fish, it is every pelican for itself. White pelicans, in contrast, are quite dependent upon each other. Paddling on smooth water, they usually fish in a loose circle or line. The swimming pelicans herd and even surround schools of fish, often driving the fish toward shore or shallower water. Then the pelicans sweep their huge pouches into the schools. A fish that escapes the lunging pouch of one pelican may not be so lucky with the next. By fishing together—scientists call this unusual behavior **communal** or cooperative—the pelicans can keep a school of fish trapped among them.

Above: *Brown pelicans fish alone.*
Below: *American white pelicans work together to surround schools of fish and sweep them into their bills.*

Most brown pelicans spend their lives close to home.

MIGRATION

As a general rule, brown pelicans spend their lives fairly close to where they were born. Some groups of them, however, fly a few hundred miles (several hundred km) north or south, depending upon the season and the availability of fish. Some California-born brown pelicans, for example, travel north along the Oregon coast in summer.

White pelicans, on the other hand, take very predictable, long-distance journeys called **migrations.** Except for the colonies in Mexico, white pelicans travel south each fall to escape winter and north each spring to reach nesting grounds. Some of these migratory journeys are more than 2,000 miles (3,200 km) long!

White pelicans leave their northern lakes to spend the cold winters on southern shores.

White pelicans cannot tolerate extreme cold, and the ponds, lakes, and marshes where they fish each spring and summer become ice covered. In fall the birds' urge to migrate south is triggered by seasonal changes, such as cooler temperatures and ever-shortening periods of daylight. By leaving nesting grounds shortly after the young birds have begun to fly, the pelicans have several weeks to travel south in reasonably good weather.

Autumn brings high-flying clouds of white pelicans to southern California, Florida, Louisiana, Texas, and Mexico. White pelicans that nest west of the Rocky Mountains generally winter along the Pacific Ocean. Those from colonies east of the Rockies spend winter along or near the Gulf of Mexico. White pelicans leaving Montana nesting grounds in September, for example, usually arrive at their winter homes on Florida's west coast in late October or early November.

And in spring, with days lengthening, temperatures warming, and nesting instincts becoming strong, white pelicans lift off from their wintering sites and head north. The pelicans rest at lakes and marshes along the migration path.

A young white pelican doesn't instinctively know where to go on a migratory flight. But following along as part of a flock, many of whose members have been on earlier migration journeys, the young pelican learns its route. Over time, young pelicans become old pelicans and pass on the migration routes to the next generation.

One of the thorniest questions scientists ponder about migration is how even the experienced birds find their way. A migrating pelican—or any bird—must know where it is and where it is going. It must be able to **navigate,** or find its way, and it must know when it has reached the "home" destination. Scientists have several theories about how migrating animals navigate. It is possible that white pelicans, among other birds, have a sense of direction and a memory for landscape features, like river valleys, forests, and shores. Then they use their keen eyes to help them find their way.

In spring, as the days become warmer, American white pelicans again head north.

Brown pelicans use twigs to make nests in trees or shrubs.

NESTING

Brown and white pelicans generally find nesting places in the spring. California brown pelicans, for example, begin to lay eggs in March. Most brown pelicans in Florida nest in late spring. However, some Florida brown pelican colonies don't nest until autumn or winter.

Brown pelicans along the Florida coasts usually make nests of sticks. They build their nests in trees or shrubs on islands in coastal bays. On treeless islands, such as those off the coasts of California and Mexico, brown pelicans build nests on the ground, using plant material and a few feathers.

White pelicans usually nest on flat, open islands in shallow lakes. In a few places they nest on long fingers of land called peninsulas. Their nests often consist of little more than a few feathers and leaves or stems set in a scraped-out hollow. Some white pelicans build their nests in marshes on floating mats of vegetation. Nests surrounded by water, whether floating or on islands, usually offer pelicans safety from land **predators,** animals that hunt them for food, such as raccoons, skunks, and coyotes.

Nesting colonies of both brown and white pelicans typically hold 50 to 1,000 pairs. The colonies are crowded, and they reek of dead fish. But the smell is bothersome only to human visitors. Pelicans, like most birds, have little or no sense of smell. Colonies are noisy, too. Young pelicans squawk, croak, and bleat like lambs.

Large groups of white pelicans nest on islands in a lake or on protected fingers of lakeshore.

Pelicans often share nesting islands with other colonial birds, such as egrets, herons, cormorants, and gulls. Just which species join a pelican colony depends on the location of the nest site. Adult bird neighbors on the islands are not real threats to each other, although squabbles are common because nests are close together. A trespassing bird can earn a jab from a neighbor's beak, but the only serious conflicts are with gulls. California gulls, for example, are quick to eat the unattended eggs of their neighbors, including those of pelicans. Gulls will also peck small, unguarded pelican chicks to death. Still, gulls can be useful neighbors for their timid colony mates, such as the pelicans. Noisy and aggressive, gulls dive at any predator that approaches a colony.

Gulls are dangerous neighbors because they will eat unguarded pelican eggs. But they are also noisy and aggressive and will drive off other predators.

A brown pelican's drab plumage becomes bright yellow, bone white, and reddish brown during nesting season. The skin around its eyes turns red.

At the onset of the nesting season the **plumage,** or feather covering, of pelicans undergoes amazing changes. Brown pelicans are drab in their gray-brown and white plumage for much of the year. But as brown pelicans begin courtship and nest building, their heads become bright yellow and their necks as white as old bone. Later, their necks and breasts turn deep reddish brown below their yellow cap, and the skin around their eyes turns to red.

White pelicans in the nesting season show off fancy, yellow-tinged crests and yellow-trimmed breast feathers. Their feet and pouches turn Popsicle red and orange. The most striking change in the white pelican, however, is the curious knob or rhinolike "horn" that grows atop its upper mandible. The American white pelican is the only pelican species with this knob. The knob may stand 3 or more inches (over 8 cm) tall, but it's a temporary ornament. When the pelican begins to incubate eggs, the knob drops off.

Ornithologists, long puzzled about the purpose of the white pelican's knob, now believe it is probably for protection. White pelicans competing for nesting sites jab at each other's beaks. The knob apparently serves as a target and shield, keeping jabs away from the soft pouch tissue.

The white pelican grows an unusual knob on its beak during nesting season. Once the eggs are laid, the knob drops off.

There are three eggs in this brown pelican nest.

RAISING PELICAN CHICKS

The beginning of the nesting season means the start of courtship between adult male and female pelicans. Pelicans use **gestures,** or body movements, like bowing and pouch displays to attract mates. Some pelicans take a mate at the age of two years, but most pelicans don't find mates until they are three years old. Scientists have no evidence that pelicans continue to take the same mate year after year. The best guess is that a pelican mates with a different partner each new nesting season.

A few days after mating, which occurs at or near the nest site, a female pelican lays her eggs, called a **clutch.** Brown pelicans normally lay two or three eggs, and white pelicans lay two. Adult pelicans must **incubate,** or warm, their eggs, by resting their warm feet and feathers on them. The mother and father pelicans take turns caring for the eggs.

Brown pelicans often care for two babies.

Brown pelicans rarely raise more than two chicks in a clutch. White pelicans rarely raise more than one. The "extra" eggs seem to be nature's insurance policy that at least one chick will survive.

Pelican babies of both species hatch after about 30 days of incubation. Pelican parents share the duties of raising offspring, and the job begins immediately. Pelican babies are born helpless and bare-skinned, so one parent or the other must keep the chicks warm. The chicks soon begin to grow a coat of tiny, fuzzy feathers called **down.** But the parents still have to warm the chicks for several weeks.

Being helpless, baby pelicans depend upon Mom and Dad for food as well as warmth. The adult pelicans **regurgitate,** or throw up, food for the chicks. For about the first 10 days, the parents regurgitate a fishy liquid right into their nest for the chicks to peck at.

Pelican babies depend on their parents for food, warmth, and shade.

After they are about 9 days old, the chicks get their food by dipping their beaks directly into a parent's pouch.

As the chicks grow, they become strong enough to get the regurgitated food by dipping their beaks directly into their parents' pouches and throats. By the time the chicks are about 9 weeks old, and nearly old enough to fly, they may weigh as much as or more than the adults. After all, by now they have gobbled up between 150 and 200 pounds (70–90 kg) of fish in their short lives. These older chicks nearly bowl their parents over as they cram their heads into the adult pelicans' mouths looking for food.

Finding fish for their young can be difficult work for the adults. For white pelicans, fishing trips are often lengthy journeys. The shallow lakes that surround the nesting colonies of most white pelicans are not always good fishing holes. Some white pelicans fly up to 100 miles (160 km) each way to reach abundant fish. Meanwhile, young chicks are cared for by the other parent.

Young pelicans, especially those raised in tree nests, are plump because they've had little exercise. Even chicks raised on the ground do little except wander around in the company of other chicks. These pelican "gangs" are called **pods,** or **crèches.** As chicks grow and develop more feathers, they spend more time in the pods and less time under their parents' breast feathers. Adults and their chicks seem to recognize each other at feeding times, apparently from sight clues such as an adult's feather and color patterns.

Older chicks spend much of their time together in pods, but return to their parents at feeding time.

LIFE AS A YOUNG BIRD

By the age of about 8 weeks, young pelicans raised on lake islands begin to swim. Their flight feathers have nearly filled in, and the youngsters often exercise their wings by flapping them. White pelicans begin to fly at 9 to 10 weeks of age, and brown pelicans are **fledged** (have their flight feathers) at 10 to 12 weeks. Newly fledged pelicans have adult size, but not adult plumage. Adult plumage, which is the feather coat of adults, takes about 3 years to fully develop.

With the ability to fly, a young pelican achieves new independence. But its independence comes with a price: it must quickly learn to feed itself. No longer does the adult feed its youngsters. A young pelican does not leave the flock when it learns to fly. By nature, pelicans roost, rest, nest, and feed in each other's company. But being able to fly is no guarantee of survival. Each individual must depend upon its own strength and skills to survive.

At 10 to 12 weeks, young brown pelicans have their flight feathers and learn to fly.

Left: *The three young white pelicans on the left will be ready to fly in another few weeks.*
Below: *In order to survive, young white pelicans must learn to fish just as these adult whites are doing in their winter home in Florida.*

A young white pelican, for example, quickly learns to fish by joining the other pelicans on their fishing trips. But it faces its own test of strength and endurance when the flock migrates south. If it cannot keep up with the flock, it will straggle behind and likely die.

A newly fledged brown pelican probably won't face long distance travel, but it must learn to dive to eat. Not all brown pelicans can master that craft, even with their instincts and the example of their elders. Yet without being able to dive, they too will perish.

For their first 2 or 3 years, young pelicans are "bachelor," or non-breeding, birds, although they remain in the company of adult pelicans until the start of the spring breeding season. Non-breeding white pelicans usually accompany the adults on their return trips north, but sometimes they remain on the wintering grounds in bachelor flocks until the next spring migration.

A young brown pelican will have to learn to dive if it is to survive.

By the time they are old enough to breed, young white pelicans may seek a new nesting area if the old one is too crowded. Unlike some wild animals, pelicans are fairly **adaptive.** If a former nesting area is too crowded or has deteriorated for some reason, pelicans move elsewhere to set up housekeeping. In recent years, for example, white pelicans have expanded their nesting range eastward into Wisconsin, where they had not been living since the beginning of the 1900s. And they have been seen looking over a possible nesting site in Michigan.

Young pelicans that survive migration and master fishing skills have at least the chance of living long lives. One brown pelican was known to have lived 31 years.

PELICANS AND PEOPLE

Because they live close to busy seaside cities, brown pelicans are often trusting of people and even bold. The birds have learned that people and their boats can be sources of food. At hundreds of American docks where anglers (people who fish) toss fish and bait scraps into the sea, brown pelicans scramble after them. Some brown pelicans have learned to steal bait from fishing buckets and baitfish from fishers' lines. Pelicans are often hooked and injured when they raid fishing lines. Unfortunately, they don't seem to learn from their experiences. Anglers report reeling in pelicans with a dozen rusty fishing hooks still in their bills and pouches.

Brown pelicans that live near coastal towns have become used to people. These pelicans are waiting for fish scraps.

Pelicans hang around fishing boats, waiting for fish remains to be thrown away.

White pelicans are generally more wary of people. But even they will swim close to boats and fish-processing plants when fish remains are thrown out.

North America's pelicans have prospered in recent years. The populations of both species have increased, and pelicans have begun nesting in new locations.

Not too many years ago, though, the prospect of pelicans increasing their numbers seemed dim. In the 1920s, the U.S. government, now the guardian of most pelican flocks, organized the killing of white pelicans in Yellowstone National Park. The pelicans, anglers complained, were catching more cutthroat trout than they were, and the government acted out of concern for the anglers. Some years later, pelicans faced a much more serious threat: the effects of DDT.

DDT is a powerful **pesticide,** or insect-killing chemical. After World War II (1939–1945), it was applied widely on crops in the United States.

But DDT killed more than insects. The pesticide slowly washed from crops and fields into waterways, like the Mississippi River. The tiny fish and other creatures that absorbed the chemical from the water were eaten by larger fish. The flesh of the larger fish became a storehouse for the pesticide. When fish-eating birds—especially ospreys, bald eagles, and brown pelicans—ate fish poisoned with DDT, the birds, too, were affected.

DDT rarely killed birds directly, but it caused their eggs to have unusually thin shells. Some eggs cracked open as they were laid. Others cracked under the adult birds' weight. That resulted in extremely low nesting success for birds that regularly ate fish contaminated with DDT. By 1961 the brown pelicans of Louisiana, "The Pelican State," had disappeared. The U.S. Fish and Wildlife Service soon listed the brown pelicans of the United States as **endangered,** or at risk of disappearing from the country.

DDT, a powerful pesticide, caused the eggs of pelicans and other fish-eating birds to weaken, so fewer babies hatched.

In 1972 the U.S. government banned most uses of DDT. Since then, the pesticide has steadily disappeared from the environment, and the populations of bald eagles, ospreys, and brown pelicans have dramatically increased. The brown pelicans of the United States are no longer threatened. By 1999 Louisiana had nearly 50,000 brown pelicans, the result of a 13-year restocking program bringing brown pelicans from Florida.

Pelicans still face dangers, of course. Some are quite natural, like the occasional thievery of eggs and small chicks by predators and the destruction caused by hurricanes. People's actions create other, more far-reaching dangers for fish-eating birds. Chemical spills and water pollution, for example, are ongoing problems. In some coastal countries, a shortage of fish because of overfishing by the local anglers is a real problem for pelicans, but so far not in North America. But even in North America boaters and anglers can cause problems when they harass pelicans. And hundreds of brown pelicans are killed or injured each year after becoming entangled in fishing line.

Hundreds of brown pelicans are killed each year when they become entangled in fishing lines.

Nearly all brown and American white pelicans in the United States and Canada are protected by law.

Water level changes also affect pelicans and other colonial birds. When people use dams to control water levels, higher levels can flood nests, and lowered levels may create land bridges that give predators a way into the bird colonies.

People in North America once saw the decline of pelican populations. But today nearly all the pelican colonies in Canada and the United States are protected by law. Former president Theodore Roosevelt would be proud. It was he who established, in 1903, the first national wildlife refuge in the United States, Pelican Island. It protected a colony of brown pelicans in Florida.

Today the United States has a magnificent chain of wildlife refuges and wetlands that protects not only the nesting colonies and migratory stopovers of pelicans, but the habitats of hundreds of kinds of other wild animals as well.

It looks like "goin' fishin'" will continue to be a way of life for North America's pelicans for a long, long time.

Pelican populations are thriving, and it looks as if pelicans will be fishing in North American waters for a long time.

GLOSSARY

adaptive: able to change

clutch: the eggs laid in one nest

colony: a nesting area where many birds of the same species nest together

communal: living and working together

crèche: a group of growing chicks that flock together

down: short, fuzzy feathers

endangered: at risk of disappearing forever

estuaries: the waters where rivers meet the sea

fledged: having grown flight feathers

gestures: body movements

incubate: to warm and care for an egg until it hatches

insulate: to protect from cold and wetness

lunge: a sudden jab with a beak

mandible: either the upper or the lower part of a bird's beak

migration: a seasonal long-distance journey

navigate: to follow a route

ornithologist: a scientist who studies birds

Pelecaniformes: the scientific name

for the group of birds that includes pelicans

pesticides: chemicals that kill insects

plumage: all the feathers on a bird

pod: a group of growing chicks that flock together

predators: animals that kill and eat other animals

preen: to clean, oil, and arrange feathers

regurgitate: to throw up food

species: a group of animals or plants that share similar characteristics and can breed together

INDEX

ABOUT THE AUTHOR

Lynn M. Stone is an author and wildlife photographer who has written more than 400 books for young readers about wildlife and natural history. Mr. Stone enjoys fishing and travel and of course photographing wildlife. He is a former teacher and lives with his family in St. Charles, Illinois.